The Stranger World

For John Garvey,
with gratitude for your interest in the arts
and warmest wishes —

Pax tibi,

The Stranger World

Ryan Wilson

Measure Press

Evansville, IN

The Donald Justice Prize is sponsored by the Iris N. Spencer Poetry Awards at West
Chester University. The Iris N. Spencer Poetry Awards were created in 2005 through
the generosity of Kean Spencer, a successful businessman and benefactor of the arts.
The awards honor his mother, Iris N. Spencer, and recognize the important role of
the arts and letters in American life. Under the auspices of the Iris N. Spencer Poetry
Awards, the Donald Justice Prize was created as a national poetry award in memory of
acclaimed poet Donald Justice.

Published by
Measure Press
Evansville, IN

9 8 7 6 5 4 3 2 FIRST PRINTING

ISBN: 978-1-939574-20-6

Donald Justice Poetry Prize series production: VJB/Scribe

Cover image: Gustave Doré, *Inferno I, 1*

Also thou shalt not oppress a stranger: for ye know the heart of a stranger, seeing ye were strangers in the land of Egypt.

EXODUS 23:9

ACKNOWLEDGMENTS:

Thanks to Chelsea Rathburn, R.S. Gwynn, Rob Griffith, Paul Bone, the West Chester University Poetry Center, and everyone at Measure Press for giving this stranger a home. I'm grateful for all the friends and teachers who have supported me and who have helped in the creation of this book, and I owe a particular debt of gratitude to Austin Allen, Chris Childers, the late Judith Ortiz Cofer, Clay Cogswell, Frank Gallimore, John Irwin, Brad Leithauser, Emily Leithauser, Sabrina Orah Mark, Virgil Nemoianu, Robert Pinsky, Claudia Rankine, Mary Jo Salter, Dave Smith, Ernest Suarez, the late Derek Walcott, Rosanna Warren, Greg Williamson, the late Franz Wright, and David Yezzi. Most especially I am grateful to Matthew Buckley Smith — first reader, first friend, and best man: *viriliter age et confortetur cor tuum et sustine Dominum* — and to my wife, Kelly, for her unfailing love and heroic patience.

I extend my sincere gratitude also to the editors of the following periodicals, in which some of these poems have previously appeared, sometimes in slightly altered versions.

32 Poems: "Goths"

Able Muse: "Xenia"; "Exotic Perfume"; "Stopping by a Roadhouse in the Mountains"

Beltway Poetry Quarterly: "Horace i.11"

Dappled Things: "L'Esprit de l'Escalier"; "L'Estraneo"; "In the Harvest Season";
    "Sympathetic Horror"

First Things: "The View on Waking"

Five Points: "Yo La Tengo"

The Hopkins Review: "Cryptid"; "Authority"

Iron Horse Literary Review: "After the Sonogram"

Measure: "Beatus Ille"; "Horace i.25"; "Horace i.9"

Modern Age: "Ultima Thule"; "The Pest"

The New Criterion: "Face It"

Raintown Review: "Pike County, 1980s, Evening"

River Styx: "Man at the Party"

Sewanee Theological Review: "Inner Harbor"; "Life of the Party"

Unsplendid: "The City Under Vesuvius"; "For a One Night Stand"; "To the Reader";
    "Source"; "Anactoria"; *Ballade des Pendus*"

The Yale Review: "For a Dog"

This book is for my mother,
Dr. Martha Aderholt Wilson,
and it is dedicated
AMDG

Contents

Foreword

To enter Ryan Wilson's stunning debut collection is to encounter a world, as the title suggests, of strangers and strangeness. Consider the opening of "Xenia," which imagines the arrival of an unwelcome guest:

> One day a silent man arrives
> At your door in an outdated suit,
> Threadbare and black, like a lost mourner
> Or a Bible salesman who's been robbed.
> Penniless, he needs a place to stay.

While "Xenia" imagines an actual stranger "drinking your tea, / Or standing in your clothes at the window/ Awash in afternoon's alien light," more often the poems' speakers are strangers to themselves and those they love. In "Authority," a chilling dramatic monologue, a man recounts how he and his wife began discovering anonymous sticky-notes emblazoned with a single word, *LIAR.* "Why me?" the speaker asks. "I am in no way special, or even, / As my wife's always saying, interesting." Still, he laments, "I wake up every morning knowing / I'll find another note, and something else / I don't know how to fix."

In another dramatic monologue, *"L'Estraneo,"* a man alone in Florence, literally estranged from his spouse, sees a face he does not recognize yet feels inexplicably pulled toward, a sort of spiritual doppelganger:

> It was a face I knew I'd seen before,
> A man's face, nothing much about it special,
> Except it found a kind of answer within me
> When not one of the other faces did,
> An answer like a note subsumed in its chord,
> Like someone kneeling down in front of a stream

In which his own reflection's waiting for him,
And has been waiting, though he didn't know it,
And will be there still, even when he's gone.

When he reaches the man, who speaks almost no English, while the speaker knows little Italian, he is greeted like a friend:

I stood there stunned. There's no way we could have known
Each other, yet we recognized each other.
How can you know a person you don't know?
I've not known people whom I thought I knew,
But this was even more mysterious,
Like walking in a house in a new town
Where you have never been before, and feeling
Like you grew up inside its foreign rooms,
Flooded with memories that never happened.

The sense of double-ness the speaker in *"L'Estraneo"* experiences occurs again and again in the world of these poems, a world where the past reverberates through the present, where a song that marked a brief relationship is played on a passing ringtone ("Yo La Tengo") and a man can leave the middle of a party, "the lights off, / Everyone's face in shadows, to climb the fence / And measure out my steps through deserted fields / Thirty years ago" ("Life of the Party"). That double-ness is amplified by the poems' music, by the patterns and variations afforded by perfectly chosen rhyme and meter. Working in a variety of poetic forms, from the sonnet and villanelle to *terza rima* and even the *bref double* ("Face It"), all unified by careful attention and supple lines, Wilson marries sound and sense seemingly effortlessly.

A collection containing so many forms and voices (Wilson includes skilled translations of Horace and Baudelaire in two sections labeled *Intermundia*) might feel disjointed, but that's not at all the case here. Part of the book's cohesion comes from Wilson's technical mastery, but it's also due to his clear and unifying vision. For all of his speakers' trepidation, Wilson firmly embraces the stranger without as well as the stranger within, moving from xenophobia, a fear of the foreign and unknown, to xenia, an openness to the stranger and, indeed, the world in all its imperfections and strangeness. In this wide-ranging and inclusive book, Wilson serves as the perfect guide to this stranger world.

Chelsea Rathburn

The Stranger World

I.

Stabant orantes primi transmittere cursum,
tendebantque manus ripae ulterioris amore.

VERGIL, Aen. VI. 313–314

Man at the Party

These plates and this obligatory cake. . .
These wizard dunce-caps, drolly tolerated. . .
These smiles held up, like eggs we mustn't break:
Oh, it's a fearful doom to which man's fated.

Untroubled by the great and ravening Sphinx,
No pox, no dragon causing us to quiver,
We're slaughtered by averted eyes and winks
From teenaged daughters, splashing in the river

While gossip weaves its insubstantial knit
To bind us here in this festooned pavilion,
Mouths stuffed with sweets and what we won't admit,
Amid sunlight and ribbons, aging, alien.

We are the men of inattentive shrugs
And accident, of oops and beg your pardon,
Nosing through vacuity like slugs
At home in winter's disremembered garden. . .

But now the one for whom we've come arrives.
He drifts, with sleepy mien, into our center,
And we surround him, flashing smiles like knives,
While he relinquishes the useless splinter

His father wrought him for a sword, unfazed
Among the tensed balloons, the cheer and glitter
Tomorrow's party will discover razed.
His mother watches, distant as a sitter,

As he comes into our fold, this boy of ten,
Whom I saw alone, at swordplay in the meadow,
Smiling now with manly acumen,
Done thrusting at his magnifying shadow.

After the Sonogram

Within you, now, a shadow feeds
On everything you are, and do.
Now every action scatters seeds
Across the future's fields, where you

Will watch what isn't, come to be.
The way the shadows of a field
Rise up at night, triumphantly,
And all the stuff of day's concealed,

Consumed, the hidden thing that is
Unbeing now will flourish soon,
And rustle wind-shook promises
Of goodness to a ghostly moon.

Goths

Don't listen to that ungodly racket
Your parents make about your hair, your dates,
          The spooky associates
With whom you trudge into the night, your jacket
Purposely left behind. The old debate's

Always the same. They say you're foolish
And you say they're pathetic, who've allowed
          Themselves to join the crowd
Of fleshy middle-aged folks making ghoulish
Faces when the Witch House gets too loud.

Forget them. Forget the disquisitions
Your teachers offer just to keep you bored,
          That History award
You should've won, the college's Admissions
Policy, the shrewd class-pets, and the simian horde

That rules the hallways you get lost in
The way a ghost is lost in sunlit air.
          Let your youth's baffled despair
Vanish in a fifth of Mr. Boston.
Go out into the dark, go out somewhere

With older kids who have deserted
Their futures already, who've sliced up their wrists on a bet,
          And keep a cigarette
Behind your ear for the one with whom you've flirted
In Lit. Like Romeo and Juliet,

Head out for a graveyard's shade.
Beneath the elms, you'll hear howls of mock derision,
        But hold to your decision
And lose yourself, till the human noises fade,
In heavenly pleasures, shielded by tombstones from vision.

For a Dog

You'd wake us up — that shrill, insistent bark
Driving away whatever dreams had fogged
Our vision — and we'd rise in the true dark,

Wondering just what exactly, catalogued
By canine instinct under "*THREAT*," was there,
What jogger, cat, or dog it was that dogged

You from your drowse beside the easy chair
And summoned your yapped pandemonium.
Nine times in ten it was just empty air,

Some ghosted scent you sniffed. Dumb — you were dumb,
Like all dogs, snuffling up to snakes, afraid
Of mice. When we said 'come,' you wouldn't come;

You capered when commanded to play dead,
And when we wanted most to be alone
You'd offer up that imbecilic head

Until we crowned your pity with a bone.
Our lives took on the shape you spun from need,
The harried rondure of routine. You gone,

The house is quieter, and we've been freed
Forever from the never-ending chores
Your tail entailed, the scrubbing where you peed,

The hunting stain-removers down in stores.
What's hardest are the peaceful hours we wanted
So much when you were scratching up the doors

And howling at some phantom thing that haunted
The world without, some threat we couldn't see
That you were desperate to have confronted.

Now you're part of that present unity
Of absences the living move among,
In which what was, what will, and what can't be

Dance in a ring to a triumphant song
We don't have ears to hear, or heart to see,
Who sleep now perfectly, and much too long.

Anactoria

After you die, who will remember you
Love to pass summer evenings in the shade,
The lindens green along the avenue,

Dancing to all the old songs like they're new,
Teasing boys, sipping a spiked lemonade?
After you die, who will remember you

Take home the cute ones, and their girlfriends too,
Lovers behind you strung in sad parade,
The lindens green along the avenue

As if they never had a thing to do
But shimmer resolutely, unafraid?
After you die, who will remember you?

You watch day break, and weep at the bruised blue
Of the horizon till the sun's displayed
The lindens, green along the avenue.

Days fail. Loves pass. We move on with the new.
Then it's the endless field where roses fade.
We are the dust. No one remembers you.
And the lindens still green all down the avenue. . . .

Souvenir

Now comes the autumn of the year,
When we collect the burnished leaves as they expire
And, maybe, press one in a book, a souvenir,
Then all the rest give to the fire.

When we're done with life's leaden grief,
Perhaps the future will provide us with some friend
Who'll read these days carved in the veins of a frail leaf,
And allow one to reel, once more, on the wind.

Beatus Ille

He's happiest on weekends in the fall,
      Those quiet afternoons
Of chilly light he's sure no one will call
And, in the leaves' kaleidoscopic swoons,

He lets the drowsy hours drift away.
      Brief swirls of gold and umber
Wheel past the deck where he devotes the day
To cultivating an observant slumber,

Untroubled by his work's insistent claims
      On his attention, or
His wife, away on business, or the games
On TV, young men running up the score

Desperately. There's no party to attend,
      No need for artifice.
He doesn't have to lie to console a friend,
Or give his cheek to a pretended kiss

Or feign an interest in political twaddle.
      For once, he feels, he's free,
So he presses his warm lips to a bourbon bottle
And, reminiscing, wanders aimlessly

Out through the yard, the blue-black night's cool air,
      Savoring every sip
Among the dead leaves, drifting here and there,
The half-moon smiling like a sunken ship.

II.

For the Platonic man is entirely intelligible as a rational animal, but he is not quite so intelligible as soul and body. . . Matter is there as an unreduced stranger within reality, an unintelligible and barbaric alien.

ANTON C. PEGIS

EDWARD: *Then I myself must also be a stranger.*
UNIDENTIFIED GUEST: *And to yourself as well. . .*

T. S. ELIOT, *The Cocktail Party*

Cryptid

The Carolina Black Panther

They will not believe I exist in these hills now.
    Sometimes I don't either.
My voice smothers all the summer flowers with snow —
    Where I walk the green world withers

With earth vibrating through my unworldly sinews,
    Each stride resonating
Inside me like a strummed chord's sad euphoria
    I hear somewhere far from here.

Nights I howl the gut gospel they say is the wind.
    They like their kitties small,
Trees in neat little squares of sidewalk.
    I hold death pooled in my jaws.

I stalk through shadows and deserted streets,
    The places no one goes,
And grow stronger among widowed houses
    And those schools where zeroes busted windows

And feeling huge as night I heave myself back home
    To the hills and to my cave.
Sometimes a child will find the dark candelabra
    Of my track in the mud

And follow it into the woods' green blackness.
                If he is brave he'll hear
The cave's mumble under the river's hush,
                The sound of shadows breathing,

And return to town to tell the others and be ignored.
                Alone he'll pull his blanket
To his throat, his body lost underneath clean sheets,
                A little ghost haunting himself.

If he is a god he will go beyond the cave
                And the river to where
There are no sounds or shapes or smells or thoughts,
                The place the dead live, and live there

Beyond the need for love, for being understood.
                I know it's there. I live nearby.
I keep descending in the darkness from the woods
                So he might come, and I can die.

Lullaby for a Suburban Summer Evening

When the wind-up figurines wind up on dusty shelves,
And the lamplight pins shadow-butterflies up against the walls,
And the silence extends to us a presentiment of unknown selves
And the evening we have begged for all day quietly falls;

When, over the chimneypots, the bats go flitting by
And fireflies wheel brief constellations through the yard;
When the clock's chipped new shapes from the marble alibi
And the hackers have maxed out another Discover card;

When the uneaten food rots in the glutted garbage bin
And the rabbit unearths nuts squirrels hid in the flowerbed,
And the last light circles the horizon like a savage fin,
And smoky tresses undulate around the world's untroubled head;

When the Gmail account can offer us no new messages
And the laptop, and the children, are falling asleep;
When the pulse of the crickets is all that there is,
And, through open windows' curtains, the astral breezes sweep,

And the house is no shelter, but only brick and wood,
And the barflies keep drinking more drinks till their throats parch,
When tranquility sifts down on the drowsy neighborhood
You can hear, if you're quiet, the dark night on march.

Face It

A silence, bodied like wing-beaten air,
Perturbs your face sometimes when parties end
And, half-drunk, you stand looking at some star
That flickers like a coin wished down a well,
Or when you hear a voice behind you whisper
Your name, and turn around, and no one's there.
You're in it then, once more, the stranger's house
Perched in the mountain woods, the rot-sweet smell
Of fall, the maples' millions, tongues of fire,
And there, whirl harrowing the gap, squint-far,
That unidentified fleck, approaching and
Receding at once, rapt in the wind's spell —
Pulse, throb, winged dark that haunts the clean light's glare —
That thing that you're becoming, that you are.

The City Under Vesuvius

The day you learn New York does not exist,
London will be erased, and Paris missed,
And everything you've known — the pottery,
The fruit, the windows and high-rises — will be
Reduced to blackened flecks, and on that day
You'll find no breath can wheeze them all away.
There's nothing you can pack, no cab to call.
Walk out the door of yourself, love, leave it all.
I'm waiting every place you can't quite see.
Sweet corpse, Pompeii is not in Italy;
It's just below the surface of the lake
You've looked so long into to watch your fake;
Beneath the cloak, beneath the mask, the face
Of something nameless, a place without a place.
Come live under Vesuvius, my dear,
My life. The skeletons wish you were here
Where ancient hammers still in mid-strike ring,
Cold forges crackle and untouched irons sing.
Here nothing moves, and nothing ever dies.
Young Icarus is plastered in these skies,
Arched upward, far beyond the fatal heat,
And here's the famous labyrinth of Crete.
Here life is led inside its death. We live
Shaped by our knowing it, a negative
Where shadows show up white and light is dark,
Where nothingness finds snow in every spark.
Come quickly. We'll, unmoving, walk the street
Where lava seethes forever beneath our feet
And sweetest char and ash coat everything —

The stars and sky, peach-blossoms in the spring,
Mountains and streams and fields and you and me —
Holding our shapes for all eternity
In vivid forms beyond the touch of age,
Dark ink carving words from a blank page.

Authority

When the notes started, I knew something was off.
The whole thing just felt so weird. I'm not the type,
You understand, who wanders around searching
For signs from some invisible world, reading
Clues into swallows' migratory patterns
Or decoding the secret meanings hidden within
Cracks in the sidewalk. I'm not the kind who suffers
From visions or shamanic revelations,
And I don't shout down people on the street
Or carry an apocalyptic sign
Or anything. I voted Democrat
And do my nine-to-five like everyone else,
Which is precisely why it doesn't make sense.
 Why me? I am in no way special, or even,
As my wife's always saying, interesting.
The doctors can't even hide their boredom from me
When they come in with their charts held to their chests
The way, in movies, you see old-timey preachers
Carrying Bibles. They say I'm fine, and try
To smother a sigh, and say to get some rest.
And that's what's wrong, really: that nothing's wrong,
And yet I wake up every morning knowing
I'll find another note, and something else
I don't know how to fix.

                    The whole thing started
When JoAnn — that's my wife — told me about
The lamp in the back bedroom. It didn't work,
She said, so naturally I went and changed

The bulb. Nothing. I checked the plug, and tried
Another outlet. Nothing. The thing was dead.
Of course, I'm not the handy type — a fact
Of which JoAnn constantly reminds me — so
I told her not to worry, that I'd take it
To someone who could fix it. Thing is, they couldn't.
So off to Sears I go and buy another
And bring it home, and set it up, and: nothing.
I told her I'd take the damned thing back in the morning.
But when we got up, we were drinking our coffee
And kind of roaming through the house to open
The curtains up as usual, when we noticed
The note. A sticky-note, hand-written, black ink,
There on our new lamp's patterned white shade.
What did it say? It said, *LIAR*. Can you believe that?

I'll tell you now, we didn't know what to think.
JoAnn, of course, assumed the thing meant me
(As if she never told a lie), and starts in on me
With questions. Do I have a girlfriend? Have I
Been sneaking drugs? Am I a compulsive gambler?
I told her that she knew as well as I did
I'm home with her every night, and eat with her
And go to bed with her and fall asleep
Watching *Fallon* with her. She gave me a look,
Like maybe I had figured out the trick
To being in two damned places at the same time,
Like I'm the type who just *would* have masterminded
Some magical scheme to wiggle out of the laws
Of physics in order to get away with something
Devious. I told her I hadn't done anything
And she knew it. And then I kind of wondered

If maybe she had been living a secret life
But I knew better than to poke that dragon.
The question then was: who had left the note?
I surely didn't know, and hated to think
What it would mean if JoAnn somehow knew.
She said she didn't, and, well, I believed her.
So we said *kids,* and then *intruders,* turning
Our talk toward an analysis of how
Socio-economic pressures cause
Everyone in capitalist cultures
Problems, as those oppressed through poverty
Cannot be seen in isolation from
Those who oppress them, and the crimes committed
By the oppressed in desperation are,
Ultimately, only natural reactions,
Of opposite but equal force, to the hushed crimes
Committed by those who are their oppressors.
We didn't know what else to say about it.
A mutual sigh. We let it go at that,
And then got dressed, and went about whatever
The business of the day was.

                      The new new lamp
Didn't work either, and the next week, when
The electrician came, he didn't see anything
Wrong in the wiring. We tried to shrug it off,
And we had almost forgotten about the note,
After about a month, when I got home
From work one evening and found JoAnn there sitting
Alone at the dining-room table in the dark.
No dinner smells, no plates laid out, no greeting.
I was afraid to ask. It was JoAnn,

I knew — I've known her ever since high school —
But there was something different about her,
A kind of quietness to her, a radiating
Silence that engulfed me and strangled the voice
Inside my throat, the way the statues of saints
In church, back when my mother made me go
To mass with her, would seem to radiate
A hush throughout the nave, so that it seemed
To require a great effort in the lungs to muster
A whisper, like trying to have a conversation
Under water. I was afraid to talk,
And she just sat there like a statue, and weirdly
She seemed to me in that darkness more lovely
Than she had been in years, not like these girls
In their bikinis on the magazines
But like those women that the old painters
Put down as nymphs or obscure goddesses
In such a way you almost believe the women were
Secretly immortal, and only the painter saw it.
Then, out of the subaqueous dark in that room,
A sound it took a second for me to realize
Was her voice came, and I was so surprised,
As if a mermaid or the mouth of a cave
Had just posed me a question, I had to ask her,
Whisperingly ask her, to repeat herself.
Another silence, long enough to crawl inside,
And then her voice again, asking, *What is this?*

I had, of course, like a fool, started flipping
All the light-switches when she reached her hand out.
The note, she said, had been taped up inside
The fuse-box in the basement. You know, *LIAR.*

We knew there was no point before we tried
The electrician, but we tried, a bunch of companies.
The last one rewired the whole house: still nothing.
Our friends told us to move, and we hoped to,
But the real estate agents said there was no use
In listing the house, especially since, by this time
It wasn't just the lights. JoAnn had opened
The dishwasher when it wouldn't run one night
And found a note. And then the kitchen sink
One morning, a yellow sticky on the faucet.
We put in several calls to the Sheriff's Department
And got some deputies to stay on watch
Outside the house, but nothing seemed to help.
Our cars stopped running, little notes stuck on
The steering wheels. Then our computers at work.
Neither of our bosses felt too good about it,
And they were surprisingly kind, but we understood
When they said they didn't have much choice about
Letting us go. It was around that time
We did move to a smaller place, an apartment,
And started seeing doctors. But nothing was wrong
With us, they said, and when the process began
Repeating at the apartment — the lights, the water,
And always the notes — we started to accept
That this is just the way life sometimes goes.
After all, the local farmers had a drought
To deal with, no doubt due to global warming,
And cows were falling dead out in the fields
From some new bug, dozens a day they said,
And the town's factories were constantly
Closing down, leaving people worse off than ourselves,
So even with the dual housing payments

And our savings leaking like the damned Titanic,
We started to adapt, and everything
Might have kept going on like that and been
Ok, except this thought that I kept having.
I couldn't sleep because this thought nagged at me,
Like a dog scratching at the door to be let in
Or a baby in another room, crying all night —
The thought that, since I hadn't done a thing
That could have brought about such consequences,
JoAnn must know more than she'd said about it.
There was no other rational explanation:
She must know something, must have done *something*.

I knew enough about being a good husband
Not to ask her about it. Put her on the spot
And she just gets upset, and I don't blame her:
I don't like being interrogated either.
At first I just spent a lot of time in the dark
Living-room, drinking whisky with store-bought water
And thinking through what I knew as the facts of the matter.
The whisky had no effect (there'd been a note),
But it seemed part of the Sherlock role I was playing,
So I'd drink whisky until time for bed,
And then, when she was asleep, I'd tiptoe out
And delicately explore what was inside her bag
With no real notion of what I was looking for,
But a sense that there simply had to be something to find.
There wasn't. Nothing in her closets, either,
Or hidden in her clothes, or in her shoes,
Or our increasingly useless furniture,
Or even stuffed in the hardened pillows and blankets.
I did, however, in a few places, find

Some balled up bits of paper that, when unfolded,
Revealed that same handwriting, the same *LIAR*.

The night it struck me that she might have hidden
The necessary clue not in her things
But some place slightly less conspicuous,
That it only made sense she wouldn't be so stupid
As to hide the crucial clue where anyone
Might happen on it, I started thinking outside
The box, as people say. So, trying to be
Scientific and clear-eyed about the whole thing,
I concluded that the only reasonable explanation
Was that somehow something was hidden somewhere deep
Inside her. Well, far be it for me to suggest
Therapy or exploratory surgery,
And then deal with the fight, the tears, and all,
(Not that I'm one of those whack-jobs who think
Women are over-emotional or something—
There's no place in society for that type,
Or anyone who would deny the fact
That we are all the same), so for a week
Things went on more or less the way they had,
While I kept thinking how to get the thing
That she had hidden inside of her out.
And then one night, we went to bed as usual,
(Jimmy had Kim Kardashian on that night)
And when dawn's blue light seeped in through the blinds
And woke me up, I saw JoAnn was gone.
I ran my hand along the warm emptiness
Where she had been until I felt the paper
And heard its rustling sound, like wind in the trees.

A few days later, a cop called, said they'd found
Some body-parts down in the rushes there
Along the river, and they thought it was
JoAnn. By this point, I'd decided that
I couldn't trust the cops. I played along,
And said, *Yes, it must be,* and cried for them,
But I knew better. See, it couldn't be
JoAnn they found because she'd never left,
Not really anyway. When I would stand
In front of the bathroom mirror in the mornings,
Brushing my teeth, or maybe combing my hair,
I'd be sort of distracted, and then there
Behind me she'd be smiling, with a note
Held in her hand up underneath her chin,
In front of her throat. A kind of joke, I guess.
And then, all day, I'll hear her teasing me,
Or griping, in the room next to whichever
Room I'm in, and sometimes, in the night,
When I wake up and turn over, I'll open
My eyes and there she is, propped on her elbow,
Smiling at me and holding one of those notes
In her fingertips, her nails a deep red color
That seems almost to radiate in the dark,
Her body posed there in her negligee
In a way that I can only call *seductive.*
Of course, I couldn't say exactly why
She's doing what she's doing, but I'm sure
She has good reason, so I don't much worry
About it. I just focus on my work:
Nine to five, every day, and often long
Into the night, working on this secret book
I started around the time I lost my job.

The cops still call sometimes, or they'll drop by,
And ask about whatever new thing's broken—
The Mr. Coffee, the blender, the trash compactor,
Most of my tools, including the saw and the drill
JoAnn gave me for Christmas some years back—
And I will sit, and listen to them talk,
And nod, certain that their insinuations
Signal a weak-brained inefficiency
If not outright complicity in the crime
Whose repetitions have marked these days and years,
But I nod, and smile politely, while I work on
The book inside my head, making my notes.
The book's a history of religious doubt,
A kind of paean to the brave free-thinkers
And philosophical authorities
Who liberated civilization from
Despots and the Dark Ages. It's almost finished,
But I'm scared that I'll die before the end,
So these days I write almost all the time.

A Study of Reading Habits in Hell

The discontented dead, still, hearken
Unto the deathless verse of Larkin,
Until the dreams of sunlight darken.

François Villon: *Ballade des Pendus*

My human brothers who still live,
Don't turn to us with hearts of stone;
To give us pity is to receive
God's mercy for yourselves who've seen
Us five or six strung up, undone.
The flesh to which we gave our days
Has long since rotted, or fattened jays,
And we, the bones, turn dust this Fall.
No one should laugh at our malaise,
But pray that God forgives us all.

If we say 'brothers,' you shouldn't have
Disdain for the word, though we've gone
To death, and justly. You perceive
All men aren't always wise or serene.
Ask pardon for us, who are but bone,
From the holy virgin's son, and pray
That we are not beyond His grace,
Which spares us from the depths of Hell.
Let no one harass us, who've passed away,
But pray that God forgives us all.

Rain scoured us with stinging waves,
And the sun dried out and blackly shone.
The crows had at our eyes like thieves,
Tore out the beard, picked eyebrows clean.
And we are never left alone.
First here, then there, our bodies sway
In the fickle wind's unending play,

Pecked at like a thimble's shiny bowl.
Brothers, don't imitate our ways,
But pray that God forgives us all.

Prince Jesus, Lord of all You survey,
Don't let the devil make us obey.
Our accounts with him are paid in full.
Men, I have no jokes to say;
But pray that God forgives us all.

Xenia

One day a silent man arrives
At your door in an outdated suit,
Threadbare and black, like a lost mourner
Or a Bible salesman who's been robbed.
Penniless, he needs a place to stay.
And you, magnanimous you, soon find
This stranger reading in your chair,
Eating your cereal, drinking your tea,
Or standing in your clothes at the window
Awash in afternoon's alien light.

You tire of his constant company.
Your floorboards creak with his shuffling footfalls,
Haunting dark rooms deep in the night.
You lie awake in blackness, listening,
Cursing the charity or pride
That opened up the door for him
And wonder how to explain yourself.
He smells like durian and smoke
But it's mostly his presence, irksome, fogging
The mind up like breath on a mirror. . .

You practice cruelty in a mirror,
Then practice sympathetic faces.
You ghoul. Your cunning can't deceive you.
You are afraid to call your friends
For help, knowing what they would say.
It's just you two. You throw a fit when
He sneaks water into the whisky bottle,

Then make amends. You have no choice
Except to learn humility,
To love this stranger as yourself,

Who won't love you, or ever leave.

INTERMUNDIA

Horace: *Ode I.25*

Parcius iunctas quatiunt fenestras. . .

Your shutters rarely rattle anymore
With pebbles launched by young men's lusty scam
To steal you from your sleep, and now the door
    Lovingly hugs its jamb,

Though yesterday it swung quite easily
On its hinges. Now less and less you hear them crying:
"How can you sleep all night, ignoring me,
    Lydia, when I'm dying?"

You, in your turn, will weep, an aging thing
In deserted alleys, for your adulterers,
Some night when howling winds go reveling
    And a change of moon occurs

And you yourself burn with your love, and the lust
That makes the horses' mothers go insane
Rages within your rotting heart. I trust
    That, then, you will complain

The happy young men do not condescend
To touch smudged myrtle, but, to celebrate
Green ivy, give sere leaves to the east wind,
    Winter's furtive mate.

Horace: *Ode I.11*

Tu ne quaesieris — scire nefas — quem mihi, quem tibi. . .

You shouldn't ask — to know is devilry —
What end the gods have given you and me,
Leuconoë, nor should you fix your hopes
On anything you find in horoscopes.
Better, whatever comes, this suffering —
Whether Jupiter has judged he'll bring
Us future winters, or that this shall be
Our last, which now whips the Etruscan Sea
Crashing against the cliffs. Be circumspect,
Purify the wine, and, if you detect
Hopes overreaching their allotted spaces,
Trim them. Even as we talk, Time races
By us begrudgingly: seize the day,
And trust tomorrow little as you may.

Horace: *Ode I.9*

Vides ut alta stet nive candidum. . .

See how high snow's heaped on shimmering
Soracte? Now the bleak boughs bend to hold
The weight of snow packed thick and the swift spring
Is frozen solid, paralyzed by cold.

Dispel the winter's chill with logs piled high
And wide in the fireplace, then take the four-
Year-old Sabine vintage from our supply,
Dear Thaliarchus, and just let it pour.

The rest: leave to the gods. Once they have scattered
Their whirlwinds over seas that churn and thrash,
There's no commotion left to shake the battered
Cypress in its shaggy age, or the ash.

What will tomorrow bring? Try not to guess.
And, when it comes to Fate, count anything
You're given profit. Don't hold contemptuousness
For love and sweetness and dancing in a ring

While you're still green, and brokenhearted gray
Remains far off. Now's for the square, the park,
Secrets whispered softly as the day
Comes to its finish and dusk fades to dark,

Now is the time for laughter's treachery
To give up where, in the shadows and the mists,
That girl is hiding, for plying a ring free
From an arm, or a finger that, wickedly, resists.

III.

Or ti puote apparer quant' è nascosa
la veritade alla gente, ch' avvera
ciascuno amore in sè laudabil cosa;
però che forse appar la sua matera
sempr'esser buona ; ma non ciascun segno
è buono, ancor che buona sia la cera.

DANTE, *Purg.* XVIII, 34–39

Ultima Thule

sonetto caudato

The winter doesn't want her pale perfection
Broken. Her ice-fields shine with candied frost.
The milky pond will harbor no reflection
Of what the earth's determined must be lost,
And snow-white birches stand like patient brides
Within a blizzard quiet as a dream,
And wait to be kissed, or not, as she decides.
A white fog hangs above a lifeless stream.
Snow flurries lift and settle back, like doves,
While, given to her crystalline safekeeping,
Skeletal elms bow deeply in their groves.
Life holds the ghostly posture of the sleeping,
And the land grows silent, hushed by a snapping wind
Sweet as the peace we're promised in the end.
             But underneath the snows
That would erase a man's footstep, or his trail
Of blood, with the worm, the maggot, and the snail
             Something horrible grows,
Something moving through the land, and flooding
Buried things, like light, like sugar, budding
             In the raucous calls of the crows,
Enchanted with the music wolves make of
The hunt, a darkness, rising, merciless as love.

Inner Harbor

You've found real shores across imagined seas
And kindled in the sand, where black suns set,
The flagrant language of the mysteries,
Your cane a wand, your self the amulet:
Bravo! — It's meaningless. On every shore
The same winds whistle and the same waves hiss.
Everywhere you go is Baltimore,
A salt breeze billowing the stench of piss —
Swayback girls drowsing in their slow deceits
Like charmed cobras, and the lean boys with knives
Plotting, bass pulsing cacophonous big beats,
Rose-eyed drunks contemplating dead-end lives
Down by the shoreline where, through these dark nights,
The empty boats glow with the water-lights.

For a One Night Stand

Again lamplight cheats time and space.
Pressed to your window there's a face
Like mine, suspended in the night
Where cars lean into slanted sleet,
Scanning the warmth and wreckage of this room
While, lost in a cloudburst of perfume,
Already done with us, hair tied,
Mascara, rouge, and lip-gloss plied,
Fixing that ice-white negligee
Just before the turn away
From the mirror and the vanity
You glance, reflecting, at the bed, and me.
But, in that dubious windowpane,
Another face appears again.
And this one, equally my own,
Is drawn by some distraction
Away from you, from the bed where we
Thumbed through a battered *Odyssey*. . .
Out to the street, and across the park,
Snow shimmering, wind-blown through the dark,
To this place, removed by miles and years,
Where nothing ever disappears
And I am still as I was then,
Looking out and looking in,
Sure only what is mine to love
Is never quite the life I live.

Yo La Tengo

That indie hit
We loved the Spring
We met, and split,
And everything

Careered in two,
Doubling the pain
We singly knew,
On a tunnel-bound train

Comes thin and sappy
From someone's phone
(Dance tune to the happy),
Whose tinny ringtone

Stirs ghostly feet,
As the seconds slow,
And strangers repeat
Hel*lo*? and Hel*lo*?

L'Esprit de l'Escalier

πάντα γὰρ καιρῷ καλά.

SOPHOKLES

If your descent, that day, implied assent
And solidarity with those who hide
Amid cocktails and clever argument
From that great Truth that shall, you know, abide,
If it allowed you to play innocent
Of your convictions, if it meant you lied,
That might explain the echoes in your ears,
Your own footfalls resounding through the years.

You hear them, still, and laughter overhead,
Giggling of frivolous gods and goddesses
Pealing like thunderclaps. Where you have fled,
Against the odds and endless odysseys
That should have left the dead to tend the dead,
Those sounds return. Was it false modesty,
Fear, or a wish to live life unopposed?
The moment passed. You left. The door was closed.

That door is closed. But you're still standing there
When your eyes close, and you would go to sleep,
Still looking up, foot poised on the fifth stair
To go back, tell them. . .what exactly? Deep
Into the night, you thrash those debonair
Fools, as Ajax among the slaughtered sheep,
Naked, blood-soaked, tent lurid in firelight,
Whipped corpses, whipped, whipped, unappeased, all night.

Dream's armor's lost, Athena too, and Troy.
Dawn blazes now. You are yourself in France.
The mingled sounds of cars and birds destroy
The night's perfections: life deals just one chance.
Go down. It's time. In the streets, hoi polloi
Resume their patterns in the ragged dance
Of Spring. Never will pain, or joy, relent:
Go down, down where dissent dies for ascent.

L'Estraneo

In Florence, this past summer, I woke up
Early one Saturday and found myself
Walking on the *lungarno* to the south
With no real destination in my mind,
So when I'd reached the Ponte Grazie
I made a right on Via San Niccolo
And followed sunlit cobblestones uphill
To climb the thousand ancient stairs
That lead to San Miniato on the mountain.
I couldn't say what made me go that way
Of all the possible ways I might have gone.
(My analyst suggests a fear of death
Disguised as a desire to remain youthful,
Or maybe Masochism, but that's not it
So much as there was something eerie
About the way the Arno held the light
That morning; it reminded me of how
The singers at the Badia harmonize
Around a note, and how their hymns will rise
In calcareous light slanted from high windows,
The echoes like the incense hanging there
In whirled clouds. But I can't explain it now.
Just something about music and altitude.)

Anyway, that walk's rough, with the uneven
Stone of the stairs ascending endlessly,
It seems, gray stone on gray stone, up and up,
Relentlessly, almost vindictively,
And as I lumbered up, sweaty and winded,

Wondering why I didn't just turn back,
My quads and hamstrings burning with the effort,
I got the feeling I was being followed,
The way you feel when someone's in the room,
Or you wake up if thieves break in your house,
Even if you can't hear them: you just know
Someone is there. That's sort of how it was.
I'd stop, turn. No one would be there behind me,
And I'd keep going, then I'd stop and turn
Again, and still nobody would be there,
And I'd go on, but there was this excitement,
This thrill of terror mixed with eagerness,
Like just before you ask your boyhood crush out,
Or that split-second just before a punch
Gets thrown, almost a sense of trespassing,
Of having crossed a boundary, of being
An interloper in a stranger world
Where you've committed some crime unknowingly.
So I kept walking, for whatever reason,
And tried to distract myself from that sensation,
Admiring the shadow-play along the walk
The black-green boughs of overhanging trees
Put on, and how, along the stone wall there
On the left, roses hang, caught in the air
Like spume from a red wave breaking against a levee,
Or like kids, suspended in mid-vault above
A fence they're leaping to escape some vicious
Neighbor or dog chasing them from the garden.
Finally I reached the Piazzale Michelangelo,
Where that fake David gazes down on Florence
As if he were staring down some invisible
Giant from Gath in the Valley of Elah,

And I was following his gaze and trying to see
The way he saw when, amid the crowd
Of tourists snapping selfies in the square,
I saw a face I recognized, although
To say I recognized it isn't quite true.
It was a face I knew I'd seen before,
A man's face, nothing much about it special,
Except it found a kind of answer within me
When not one of the other faces did,
An answer like a note subsumed in its chord,
Like someone kneeling down in front of a stream
In which his own reflection's waiting for him,
And has been waiting, though he didn't know it,
And will be there still, even when he's gone.

Who was he? No clue. Didn't know a soul
In Italy. In fact, I'd fled the dissolution
Of my second marriage, and the desolation
Of its sequel, in Florence to avoid the painful
Encountering of familiar faces,
The way that, after putting on some weight,
You hide the scale from yourself, or that you stop,
As you get older, looking in the mirror
When you stand at the sink to brush your teeth,
Or that you don't much want to think of death
While in the midst of sex. Anyway,
I wasn't crazy about anyone
I'd left behind back in the States, since most
Everyone sided with my wife, not me,
And normally, however much my friends
Annoy me, they're a thousand times more pleasant
To be around than any stranger is.

(I'm terrified of strangers, terrified,
The type that, at the office party, hides
Inside the closet just to keep from talking
To vague acquaintances and unknown drunks
Who think, mistakenly, that their own wish
To talk engendereth your wish to listen.)
And yet, I walked up to this man, not knowing
What I would say, or how, but somehow knowing
I had to try to find out who he was.
The really weird thing is he seemed to know me.
When I had walked up to him, his eyes brightened
With recognition, and he clasped my shoulder
With his right hand, and kind of shook me amicably,
Like we were old friends, and he smiled at me.
But when I tried to talk to him, he just wagged
His head apologetically and mumbled
Solo Italiano. I don't have much
Italian, and it was quickly clear he had
Even less English. Still, he clasped my shoulder
Again, and smiled, and then turned and walked away,
As if he were my father, and we'd spoken
Intimately for some time, or we now shared
Some understanding I didn't know about.
I stood there stunned. There's no way we could've known
Each other, yet we recognized each other.
How can you know a person you don't know?
I've not known people whom I thought I knew,
But this was even more mysterious,
Like walking in a house in a new town
Where you have never been before, and feeling
Like you grew up inside its foreign rooms,
Flooded with memories that never happened.

The square had emptied out a little bit,
So I just stood there, looking at the sky,
A clear sort of electric cobalt color,
The light like gold-flecks woven in the blue,
As if the sky's blue and the sunlight were
The same thing, which, I guess, in some ways, they are,
Although we are accustomed to seeing them
Separately, blind as we are to the mysterious
Transition of a light into the colors
Of objects, that invisible shift that makes
The things of this world visible to us.
But as I stood there, looking down at Florence,
Rufous and khaki and brown like tesserae
In a mosaic with an abstruse pattern,
I had the sudden impulse to follow him,
This man I didn't know, this total stranger,
And took off up the path to San Miniato.
I ran. I ran a way I hadn't run
Since I was still a boy back in Poughkeepsie,
And pretty soon I spotted him ahead
Of me about a hundred yards or so,
A white shirt and a pair of khaki pants
Like half the men out there, but it was him,
I knew. I couldn't even see his face,
But I could tell. To get to him was tougher.
The lovers and the families and the cyclists
Were all out, and the path was crowded like
The crush of people when a 5k starts,
And it was hard to keep up with his pace,
But I did what I could to keep him in sight.
At San Miniato, just as I had reached
The stairs I saw him enter in the church

Above, and so I rushed up those last flights
Of stairs and stood in front of that holy place,
Green and white like snowfall over cedars,
Where Dante had studied as a young man.

Then what? Then nothing. Nothing, anyway,
I can explain. He simply wasn't there.
I wandered through the church, and through the crypt,
And through the graveyard with its crumbling stones
That mark where monks and holy men are buried.
No sign of him. I browsed around the gift-shop.
Haec est porta coeli: so I read
On a medallion there, the monastery's
Slogan. Maybe it is, I thought. Maybe
He simply passed on through that door, unseen.
Who knows? I walked back down the mountainside.

But maybe I should add another thing.
See, when I reached the square again, I heard
A tune I recognized, coming from within
A little restaurant. It was the tune
The DJ played for the last dance at our wedding.
I sat down at a table to cool off
And listened while I drank a glass of water,
And thought about my bride, warm in my arms,
How we had spun in those slow, loving circles
Out on the dance floor, all our friends surrounding
Us and spinning in their circles too,
Like planets orbiting a sun, or like
Electrons' frenzied cloud around a nucleus,
Our union holding all of them in place
For a little while, as if our love somehow

Exerted some Venusian gravity,
And I thought how our lives had come together,
How she had brought a fresh vitality
Into my days, how I had lurched toward her
The way a wasted continent will heave
Its poisoned bulk up to the verge of the sea,
How with my head upon her chest at night
I'd heard that sea flow through her veins, white birds
Winging on brisk gusts in the surf of her sighs,
Our love like that littoral, that brief shoal
On which the first impossible fish nosed up
Into the muck, set pale foot on the sand,
And vanished in the green interior.
How strange to think that such a thing had ended. . .
I was, I admit it, on the edge of tears,
And then I saw the man again. At least,
I thought I did. I can't be sure. He passed
Right by the restaurant and started down
The thousand stairs. I paid as fast as I could
And rushed out after him. It was too late.
He was gone. I never saw him again. Maybe
Because I flew home to my wife that night.
She even let me stay, although she said,
At first, she almost didn't recognize me.

The Pest

It comes to us in the night, instead of sleep,
To taunt us with the trammels of God's creatures.
Our limits ache within its quiet creep.
The muffled titter of children mocking teachers
And the wind's cold and cryptic whisperings
Whirl in its whishing shadow-movements, buried
Among our desperately dusted antique things.
Its presence, eldritch, keeps us turning, worried,
Like the off-chance we have arterial clots,
Or that we'll wake up boxed inside a grave.
Eyes shut, we try to think cool, placid thoughts:
A green shoreline, a Botticelli Love.

And still it comes, comes with weird rhythms, crawls
Somewhere unseen. We fear its touch will change
Us, make us sick. We hear it in the walls,
At its slow work, and the whole house grows strange
With childhood memories.
                                        We do not dream.
We toss like unknown planets in a void.
Inhabited silences edge us toward a scream.
We grasp each other, wild to be destroyed.

INTERMUNDIA

Charles Baudelaire: Exotic Perfume

When, with closed eyes, on a warm autumn night,
I breathe in deep the fragrance of your breast,
I see unrolling happy shorelines, blessed
With dazzling fires of an unchanging light —

An isle of indolence that nature supplies
With unfamiliar trees and fruits of rare
Savor; the men are lean and rugged there;
The women shock one with their brazen eyes.

Led by your scent into enchanted climes,
I see a harbor filled with sails and masts
Still worn out by the ocean's waves and blasts,

Meanwhile, the smell of bright green tamarinds
Is carried to the nose by circling winds
And merges in my soul with sailors' rhymes.

Charles Baudelaire: Sympathetic Horror

From that sky, livid and bizarre,
Tormented as your destiny,
Upon your dead soul what thoughts are
Descending? Skeptic, answer me.

— My hunger never satisfied
For the obscure and the unknown,
I shall not cry as Ovid cried
When banned from paradisal Rome.

You skies, like beaches torn apart,
In you my pride is mirrored back;
Your vast clouds dressed in mournful black

Are hearses for my dreamed perfections,
And your gleams flashing are reflections
Of that Hell which delights my heart.

Charles Baudelaire: To the Reader

Folly, and lies, and avarice, and vice
Possess our souls and move our limbs by force,
And we sustain our affable remorse
The way street-people fatten up their lice.

Our sins are headstrong, our atonements feigned.
We give our great confessions, doing math,
Then blithely tromp back down the mud-slopped path,
Believing our vile tears will cleanse what's stained.

Above our pillows, mystic Satan's hissed
At length to lull our dreamy heads to rest,
And the rich metal that our will possessed
Is vaporized by this shrewd alchemist.

The Devil holds the strings that move us here!
We find we're charmed by loathsome objects' spell;
Each day we take the next step down to Hell,
Crossing through putrid shades without a fear.

And like the ragged lecher who cannot
Stop mouthing on an old whore's martyred tit,
We steal clandestine thrills when we see fit,
Wringing them like an orange gone to rot.

A million swarming worms, vast companies
Of demons binge within our brains and riot,
And, every time we breathe, death slips, quiet,
Unseen, into our lungs, with a faint wheeze.

If rape and poison, arson and the blade
No longer with quaint patterns decorate
The boring canvas of our sorry fate,
It's only that, alas!, our soul's afraid.

And yet, amid the jackals and panthers, in
The throngs of vultures, spiders, vipers, apes,
And howling, grunting monsters of all shapes,
Within the zoo of our egregious sin

There's one more squalid, fierce, in a vile robe!
Unable to act, or cry, dramatically,
Still, it would have the earth made a debris,
And with a yawn would swallow the whole globe.

Boredom! — The eye unwilling tears would smother,
It puffs its hookah, dreaming guillotines.
Reader, you know this monster, how it preens —
Hypocrite reader — doppelgänger — brother!

IV.

We live in time so little time
And we learn all so painfully. . .

ROBERT PENN WARREN

Pike County, 1980s, Evening

. . .φέρεις ὄιν, φέρεις αἶγα, φέρεις ἄπυ μάτερι παῖδα.

Shadows, like secrets that the sun's concealed,
Emerge, unraveling through every field,
Weaving phantasmal nets on gravel roads
And threading paths cut through the piney woods
Where grizzled hunters and weird children roam.
The night is calling each thing to its home,
Scrawling its edicts in dark chimney smoke
That, scribbled in the mad wind, might evoke,
For college boys, the prophecies that fires
Imparted once through sacrificial pyres,
Or the tangled skeins of Ariadne's yarn.
Tools reappear on shelves in the dank barn;
The errant calves and sheep rejoin the fold.
Children stop playing, doing as they're told,
And slouch indoors to eat the evening meal
While smug hens brood on what the fox would steal;
Rifles find their way into their corners
Where they are huddled close as frightened foreigners;
The farmer leaves the furrows he's been weeding;
His wife, to set the table, lays her reading
Face-down on her armchair, so it appears
An A-frame, like those cabins on frontiers
Where lives were lived along unquiet borders;
Oh, all things settle into plotted orders
And families daylight scattered here and there
Together bow their heads, and say their prayer,
And taste the fruits they've labored to deserve.
Elsewhere, along the bypass's breakneck curve,

A handyman picks up a rag, and cleans
His fleet of irremediable machines
While formulating silent plans to do
Something, tomorrow, unforeseen, and new.
But now, the fireflies' constellations die;
Dishes are cleaned; sleep heavies every eye,
And in their fresh pajamas everyone
Slips in between crisp sheets, the good day done,
Though, through their sleep, some may yet hear
Delinquents, piled in pickups, brave with beer,
Roaring down labyrinthine back-roads with more
And more abandon, speeding, heading for
Something they can't know, whirling their brief cloud
Of dust against the moonlight, shouting loud,
As if they're being murdered, jagged screams
Gashing the night's fabric, like ghosts, like dreams.

Stopping by a Roadhouse in the Mountains

for Ernest Suarez

We parked our lives outside in the gravel
Where rusted sports-cars in rows
Nosed up to a sudden drop.
This place don't ever close,

You said. A tin-roofed eyesore, tilting
In the twilight, gradually
Acceding to gravity's patient rigors.
Knife-fights and VD

Seemed what might be called 'permanent
Fixtures', but in we went,
Vaguely lost and looking for whisky
And a way to circumvent

Risking the snaky mountain roads
In the dark. Weathered-stone faces
Turned from the bar to the door in the dim
Blue neon to appraise us,

Then vanished, like gods, within a cloud
Of smoke that, in its shifting,
Revealed three lithe girls, their eyes closed,
Swaying, sad naiads drifting

Through a song from our adolescent lives.
We ordered bourbon, then more.
No clock hung on the walls. Instead,
A mounted carnivore

Snarled with useless ferocity.
At some point the dancing girls
Grabbed us by the hands, and we forgot,
In those shambling spins and twirls,

What we wanted to forget, the damage
We were doing to our innards,
Our girls back home, work, money. . .Whatever
Wasn't in Lynyrd Skynyrd's

"Free Bird" or our drunken moves was no
Concern of yours, or mine,
Toasting our own demise and dancing
Through that dive, damned near divine.

Life of the Party

Sometimes I leave drunk dance parties, the lights off,
Everyone's face in shadows, to climb the fence
And measure out my steps through deserted fields
        Thirty years ago.

Slowly, through grass as tall as I am and gold,
Following heart-shaped tracks a deer left behind,
The river's distant sound held in a gray sky —
        Crack of a gunshot —

I make my way toward the woods that don't exist.
No beer-can pyramids. No flippant tricornes
Made out of newspaper. No gossip here or
        Skeleton costumes,

No black lights or one-night stands, wreaths of bong smoke,
Or thoughts of tank-tops and shoulders turned toward me
And women too beautiful to be human —
        Gossamer snakeskin.

I am on my dead grandparents' property.
Everything is still. Even the airplane is
Up so high it can't move. An apple tree strains
        Against abundance.

Someday I'll walk out in those pines and die there,
Wild berries in my eyes. A non-existent
Wolf will be the first and only thing to find me,
        And no one will know. . .

No. Now I'm running back, breathless, ears thrumming
With my own pulse like bass from a truck passing
Somewhere down the road, beyond the graveyard where
      All the neighbors live.

Source

The river sound was more
Than river, coming as it did from pines
And bushes, flowers, briars, and even the core,
It seemed, of earth. The signs

On the path were gibberish.
This way, the other, back. One marker, stout
And toppled, pointed skyward: "TWO MILE: FISH,"
As if heaven were rife with trout.

I tried what paths I found.
Root-stumbled, overgrown, or wide and clear,
All of them got me lost, but it seemed the sound
Boomed loudest in the ear

When I'd given up all hope
Of getting to the source. Some might have quit,
And why I didn't stop on that steep slope
And turn back, done with it,

No telling. Still, by stumbling,
Awkward, through thickets and dense underbrush,
The sky, the woods, and earth beneath me thrumming
With the river's hush,

I came to the banks at last.
For what? I cracked a beer, set my lawn chair
In the bed's muck and watched as water passed
All around me there.

I wasn't river sound
And wasn't river either, truth be told.
I was a man alone, too pleased I'd found
The water aimless and cold.

Song

I.

A gray chill, and another day,
That mausoleum atmosphere.
Drab crowds eyeball a runaway
Without a word, the city teems
With killers and hope's Ponzi schemes:
I don't know what I'm doing here.
Long shadows sweep across the mind,
And starlings fingerprint the wind.

II.

A farmhouse leans, shambolic, under
Wet cedars, and high bronze sedge trembles
While tympani of rumbling thunder
Reverberate in the dead air.
It's 1988. I'm there.
(What's real drips down from these cracked symbols.)
Wind chaps my lips. The farmhouse leans.
The fields whish. Who knows what it means?

III.

Dark cedars hung in webs of fog,
Damp split-rails sagging by the road.
A hawk hangs, whirls — fierce psychogogue
Whose motion's stillness, stillness motion.
The bleak fields sigh like a far ocean.
The whole world's waiting to explode
Into that conflagration of
Becoming Time, becoming Love.

IV.

The hawk, in ever-widening rings,
Above the ruined stubble-field,
Through gray chill, on unmoving wings,
Hunts down what it can hardly see,
Some trembling flesh crouched furtively
In fear that it will be revealed
And borne up to that altitude
Where glory gluts itself with blood.

V.

Maybe if I had seen the kill,
The carnage of the earthward dive. . .
But no, and that hawk's hanging still.
Snip-snip, the clock with its winged sheers,
And down fall gleaming days and years
But that dead hour is still alive.
As I walk by, the cafés close:
The phone-lines' staves are scored with crows.

VI.

A sourceless siren haunts the air. . .
The dead leaves' spellbound ballet twirls. . .
I'm now and then and here and there
And I'm like anyone, I guess,
Dissolved in thoughts I can't express
While, like stagefuls of dancing girls
In sequined choreography,
The stars reel through an ink-black sky.

VII.

The singers vanish in the song.
The dawn, volcanic, swallows night
And what's right's waltzing with what's wrong.
The sweeping shadows and the hawk,
The stars, the leaves, the barbarous clock,
And the faulty spirit's spiraled flight
Link rings, for now, high with the low,
The whole, the all, like awe, an *O*. . . .

In the Harvest Season

It's finished. Waiting's all that will remain.
The gossip now must go unverified.
Blue smoke from leaf-piles, smoldering like pride,
Hangs here, a ghost, a storm-cloud that can't rain.
Last night, the county's final weathervane
Fell in the high winds. Old roofs, stripped bare, preside.
Take down the ragged self you've crucified
And let the crows wing through the fields of grain.

The sagging fence will never stand up straight.
Whatever's not ripe now will never be.
That pain tormenting you will not abate,
And in the windows of vacated banks
You'll see yourself, passing by aimlessly.
You cannot change your life. Give up; give thanks.

The View on Waking

Melius enim iudicavit de malis benefacere, quam mala nulla esse permittere.
ST. AUGUSTINE

There is a kind of crypt, between
This window and the window-screen,
In which fine silken webs, unseen,

Like wires in levitating tricks,
Accumulate, somehow, and fix
Bits of the outer world: small sticks

And past years' leaves and wisps of straw
All hang, suspended in mid-fall,
Ensorcelled by some happy flaw

In joining that allowed the space
Through which stray things may find this place,
At once their tomb and saving grace,

Where gravity need not apply
And, unalive, they shall not die
As dreams do in the opened eye.

Notes

I.

EPIGRAPH: "They stand praying to put across the first watercourse, / And reach out their hands in love for the far shore." — Vergil, *Aeneid* VI. 313–14

GOTHS: "Witch House (also known as drag or haunted house) is an occult-themed dark electronic music genre and visual aesthetic that emerged in the early 2010s." — Wikipedia

BEATUS ILLE: Literally, "Happy that one": often, "Blessed is he." The title is taken from the first words of Horace's second epode. Cf. du Bellay's *Heureux qui comme Ulysse*, Sir Henry Wotton's "The Character of a Happy Life," Pope's "Ode on Solitude," etc. One may trace the *makarismos* motif back to several sources, including Homer, *Od* v. 306.

II.

CRYPTID: A cryptid is a creature whose existence cannot be, or has not been, proven by scientific means.

THE CITY UNDER VESUVIUS: Cf. Nietzsche: "Sail your ships beyond the pale and build your cities under Vesuvius."

XENIA: Xenia (ξενία in Classical Greek) is defined: "hospitality; hospitable reception or entertainment; usurpation of civic rights by an alien." (*Oxford Classical Greek Dictionary*)

INTERMUNDIA: The *intermundia*, or the "between-worlds," are the habitat of the gods in Cicero's *De Natura Deorum*. According to Epicurus, the *intermundia* (Gr. μετακόσμια or *metakosmia*) were empty spaces in the endless void.

III.

EPIGRAPH: "Now you are able to see how much the truth is hidden from the people, who believe each love in itself a praiseworthy thing, because truly its material always appears to be good; but not every seal is good, though good be the wax." —Dante, *Purgatorio* XVIII, 34–39

ULTIMA THULE: "The term *ultima Thule* in medieval geographies denotes any distant place located beyond the 'borders of the known world.'" —Wikipedia

YO LA TENGO: Literally, "I have it," or "I've got her" (Spanish). Also the name of an indie rock band, formed Hoboken, NJ, 1984, and still active.

L'ESPRIT DE L'ESCALIER: Title: literally, "the spirit of the stairs" or "the wit of the staircase": a French idiom referring to the experience of coming upon an apt response too late. Cf. Diderot. The epigraph to the poem comes from Sophokles' *Oedipus Tyrranus*, line 1516: "All things are good in their time." The *Ajax* of Sophokles is also pertinent to the poem.

L'ESTRANEO: Title: "The Stranger" (Italian). The Latin motto of San Miniato al Monte —*Haec est porta coeli*— may be rendered: "This is heaven's doorway."

IV.

PIKE COUNTY, 1980S, EVENING: The epigraph comes from Sappho's fragment 104(a) on Hesperus, the evening star, and may be rendered: "you bring the sheep, you bring the goat, you bring the child back to its mother."

THE VIEW ON WAKING: The epigraph from St. Augustine may be rendered, "For He has judged it better to make good from evil, than that evil should not be allowed to exist."

About the Author

Ryan Wilson was born in Griffin, GA, and raised in nearby Macon. He did his undergraduate work at The University of Georgia before earning an M.F.A. from The Johns Hopkins University and a second Master's degree from Boston University. His poems, translations, and criticism appear widely, in periodicals such as *First Things, Five Points, The Hopkins Review, The New Criterion, The Sewanee Review,* and *The Yale Review.* In 2015, his criticism received The Walter Sullivan Prize from *The Sewanee Review,* and in 2016 the Jacques Maritain Prize from *Dappled Things.* Currently the editor of *Literary Matters* and a doctoral candidate at The Catholic University of America, he lives in Baltimore, Maryland, with his wife Kelly.

CPSIA information can be obtained
at www.ICGtesting.com
Printed in the USA
BVOW04*0819310517

485628BV00001B/1/P